Georgia
O'Keeffe

By Barbara Buhler Lynes

RIZZOLI ART SERIES

Series Editor: Norma Broude

Georgia
O'Keeffe
(1887–1986)

GEORGIA O'KEEFFE is widely considered by critics and art historians to be one of the most important American artists of this century. Her active career began in the 1910s and continued into the late 1970s, but the paintings for which she is most well known today were completed from the mid-1920s through the 1940s. These works are characterized by subject matter that has become instantly associated with O'Keeffe—flowers, bones, and New Mexico landscapes. The forms in such paintings as *Black Iris III* (plate 5), *Deer's Skull with Pedernal* (plate 9), and *Hills and Mesa to the West* (plate 11) are clearly derived from the visible world, and this is equally true in less widely known O'Keeffes that date from this period, *Radiator Building, Night, New York* (plate 6), *Black Cross with Red Sky* (plate 7), and *White Canadian Barn II* (fig. 1), for example.

In 1916, however, when O'Keeffe's work was first exhibited by Alfred Stieglitz (1864–1946), whose innovations in photography and early support of modern art in this country are well known, it was not as obviously dependent on imagery derived from the natural world. A drawing such as *Special No. 9* (plate 2) was received by the New York art world with a mixture of suspicion and fascination. Suspicion, because the work was based in abstraction and was difficult to understand; fascination, because the artist was being touted by Stieglitz as the first woman who was willing to express her feelings in her art.

O'Keeffe had received instruction in drawing and painting as a child in Wisconsin, and by 1915 she had attended classes at the School of The Art Institute of Chicago, the Art Students League in New York, and Teachers College, Columbia University. In that year, however, she consciously rejected aspects of her formal training in order to make personal experience the subject of her art. At first she chose to express herself primarily through abstraction. Work she made then (plate 2) and into the early 1920s, such as *Evening Star III* (plate 1), *Blue and Green Music* (plate 3), and *Grey Line with Lavender and Yellow* (plate 4), documents her success at discovering a distinctively personal means of expression. Such abstractions have been recognized as among the most innovative and important produced in this country in the early twentieth century and confirm O'Keeffe's potential as an abstract painter. It is important, therefore, to consider why she did not continue to develop her art in this direction, choosing instead to produce a body of work that is dominantly characterized by immediately recognizable subject matter.

Typical of turn-of-the-century art instruction, O'Keeffe's training was centered around imitative drawing, at which she excelled. At the end of the 1905–1906 school year at The Art Institute, where the curriculum required students to copy casts of classical sculpture before attempting to draw from a model, she was awarded a commendation in life drawing by John Vanderpoel. In 1907–1908 at the Art Students League, she took a course in figure and still-life painting from William Merritt Chase, whose bravura brushwork she quickly became proficient at imitating: her oil painting *Dead Rabbit and Copper Pot* (fig. 2) won the Chase Still Life Scholarship.

Financial and family difficulties prevented O'Keeffe from furthering her education until the summer of 1912, when she enrolled at the University of Virginia in a drawing course for elementary school teachers, taught by Alon Bement (1876–1954) of Teachers College, Columbia University. Using a method devised by artist–art educator Arthur Wesley Dow (1857–1922), his colleague at Columbia, Bement instructed students to think of art as a visual harmony achieved through a synthesis of elements. He taught that individual expression should be the goal of the artist and could be realized through the selection, refinement, and arrangement of forms, without dependence on imitative drawing. The Dow approach to picture making as self-expression based on design was directly opposed to the emphasis on mimesis that had formed the foundation of O'Keeffe's training, and her adoption of Dow's principles ultimately had a profound effect on her development as an artist.

O'Keeffe experimented with the Dow method both in and out of the classroom for the next two years, while she was teaching art in the public schools in Amarillo, Texas, and at the University of Virginia, where she worked as Bement's assistant for several summers beginning in 1913. Bement introduced her to recent trends in American and European art and suggested that she read Wassily Kandinsky's influential treatise, *Concerning the Spiritual in Art* (1912), which defined art as self-expression. Moreover, Bement encouraged O'Keeffe to enroll at Teachers College in the fall of 1914, where the Dow premise that music was "the key to the other fine arts, since its essence is pure beauty" was demonstrated to her in a class of Bement's that she happened to attend.[1] Students were listening to music and, as an exercise, drawing their responses to it. As O'Keeffe recalled, "This gave me an idea that I was very interested to follow later—the idea that music could be translated into something for the eye."[2]

O'Keeffe also became increasingly attentive that year to what she called "new art."[3] She visited Stieglitz's gallery, 291, which was one of the few places in New York where examples of modern art could be seen, and she became familiar with periodicals that celebrated modernism, including

2. *Dead Rabbit and Copper Pot.* 1908. Oil on canvas, 19 x 23½".
Permanent collection Art Students League, New York

the Stieglitz-produced *Camera Work*, which featured articles about philosophy, painting, and photography, as well as reproductions of works by artists as diverse as Paul Cézanne and Francis Picabia.

It is not possible to determine how her growing awareness of modern approaches to art contributed to O'Keeffe's increasing interest in making her own experience the subject of her work, but it is clear that she had decided to seek a way of expressing herself through non-traditional means by June 1915, when she described one of her recent works as "my music," adding "[I] didn't make it to music—just my own tune."[4] And in October of that year, after she began teaching art at Columbia College in South Carolina, she made a decision about her work that set her career on its course: "[I] held a private exhibition of everything I had painted. I noticed which paintings had been influenced by this painter, which by that one. Then I determined which . . . represented me alone. From that moment forward I knew exactly what kind of work I wanted to do."[5]

Using only charcoal on white paper, O'Keeffe began a series of drawings, including *Special No. 9*, in which her primary objective was to express her feelings. In late December, she sent some of these drawings to her friend and former classmate at Teachers College, Anita Pollitzer (1894–1975), who was still taking classes there. She had already sent Pollitzer at least two other groups of her works on paper, and Pollitzer had encouraged O'Keeffe's earlier efforts that fall. In October, O'Keeffe had written to her, "I believe I would rather have Stieglitz like some thing—anything I had done—than anyone else I know of—I have always thought that—If I ever make any thing that satisfies me even ever so little—I am going to show it to him to find out if it's any good."[6] Pollitzer was so impressed with what she called "the big sort of emotions" she sensed in the drawings she received on 1 January 1916, that, in spite of O'Keeffe's admonition not to show them to anyone, she immediately took them to Stieglitz for his reaction. As Pollitzer reported to O'Keeffe, he declared:

Why they're genuinely fine things—you say a woman did these—She's an unusual woman—She's broad minded, she's bigger than most women, but she's got the sensitive emotion—I'd know she was a woman—Look at that line. . . . Tell her. . . they're the purest, finest, sincerest things that have entered 291 in a long

while [and]. . . I wouldn't mind showing them in one of these rooms one bit.[7]

There is no record of the particular work Stieglitz saw, but most of the drawings O'Keeffe made in this period are highly personal abstractions that, though probably based on landscape configurations or vegetal forms, bear little resemblance either to the visual world or to any other art that was being produced in this country in 1915. Even after decades of critical analysis (and an occasional hint from O'Keeffe) their meaning is not always clear. But there can be no doubt that O'Keeffe was obsessed in this period with the idea of creating visual equivalents of emotional states. After spending Thanksgiving of 1915 with a young man in whom she was romantically interested, she wrote to him, "I said something to you with charcoal . . . things I had no words for."[8] However, her responses to the natural world were obviously also part of what she was attempting to express. In October she had written to Pollitzer:

It's a wonderful night—I've been hanging out the window wanting to tell someone about it—wondering how I could. . . . So I thought for a long time—and wished you were here—but I'm going to try to tell you—about tonight—another way—I'm going to try to tell you about the music of it—with charcoal—a miserable medium—for things that seem alive—and sing—only I wanted to tell you first that I was going to try to do it because I want to have you right by me and say it to you.[9]

Stieglitz was particularly receptive to the drawings that O'Keeffe referred to as "the music compositions I [have] been making lately," because by 1916 he was committed to the idea that art was, above all, a response to personal experience made visual.[10] He had included several essays in *Camera Work* that addressed this issue, and in 1912 he had published excerpts from *Concerning the Spiritual in Art* as well as from Henri Bergson's *Laughter* (1911), in which Bergson proclaimed that artists should "contrive to make us see something of what they have seen. . . things that speech was not calculated to express."[11] Moreover, unlike the majority of his contemporaries, who held the traditional view that female creativity was limited to child-bearing, Stieglitz believed that women could become artists in their own right; that is, they could make art that did not imitate men's art.

By the spring of 1916, when he decided to exhibit ten of O'Keeffe's charcoal drawings in a group exhibition at 291 (see plate 2), Stieglitz apparently believed that because of the intensity of feeling he sensed in her work, O'Keeffe might be the woman artist he envisioned—able and unafraid to express herself. But he also believed that in O'Keeffe, just as in male artists, self-expression was generated by sexual feelings. He made this point clear in an essay he wrote in 1919, stating that men's and women's elemental feelings, which he considered "one of the chief generating forces crystallizing into art," were "differentiated through the difference in their sex make-up." As he explained: "Woman *feels* the World *differently* than Man feels it. . . . The Woman receives the World through her Womb. That is the seat of her deepest feeling."[12]

Thus, when he wrote about the 1916 exhibition for the October issue of *Camera Work*, Stieglitz suggested that O'Keeffe's recondite abstractions, which had created much controversy among visitors to 291, could be understood in Freudian terms: "This exhibition, owing mainly to Miss O'Keeffe's drawings, attracted many visitors and aroused unusual interest and discussion. . . . '291' had never before seen woman express herself so frankly on paper. Miss O'Keeffe's drawings . . . were of intense interest from a psycho-analytical point of view."[13] Stieglitz was a persistent advocate of his opinions, and by the spring of 1917, when he presented a selection of O'Keeffe's work from 1915–1917 at 291, his ideas about her art had been taken up by the critics who frequented his gallery. For example, one reviewer stated: "There can be no mistaking the essential fact that Miss O'Keefe [sic] . . . has found expression in delicately veiled symbolism for 'what every woman knows,' but what women heretofore have kept to themselves, either instinctively or through a universal conspiracy of silence."[14]

O'Keeffe later steadfastly denied that her work had any erotic content, but how she responded to these first published suggestions of it is not known. The idea could hardly have surprised her, however, for although she was in Canyon, Texas, where she taught art at West Texas State Normal College for two years beginning in the fall of 1916, she had been corresponding with Stieglitz since January of that year and could have had little doubt that he believed the source of her expression was her sexuality. At the same time, however, she also must have known that he was convinced hers was the first real art by a woman and that he was committed to its promotion.

In early summer 1918 O'Keeffe moved to New York at Stieglitz's invitation and, because he made it possible financially for her to devote all of her time to her art, resigned from her teaching position in Texas. She and Stieglitz began living together in the small apartment he had provided for her, and they remained together until his death in 1946 (they were married in 1924).

Their professional relationship was extraordinarily complex. Most notably, each was committed to the other's art, and there can be little doubt of mutual influences between Stieglitz's photography and O'Keeffe's painting.[15] Aside from that, however, what one was able to give the other profoundly affected their subsequent careers. For example, in her first years as Stieglitz's companion, O'Keeffe's conception of the nature of art and of her own creativity was broadened by his ideas and those of numerous American and European artists and writers who moved in and out of his circle. On the other hand, the work O'Keeffe produced vitalized Stieglitz's increasing efforts to define the nature of a uniquely American art, and along with painters Charles Demuth, Arthur Dove, Marsden Hartley, and John Marin, she was at the center of his valiant effort to win its acceptance.

After he assumed full responsibility for promoting O'Keeffe's art in 1916, Stieglitz expounded his theories about it to anyone who would listen, and the exhibitions of her work he subsequently staged were frequently controversial events in the New York art world. His promotional methods have raised many questions about his motives and about O'Keeffe's complicity in his efforts to stimulate interest. But the fact is that what he did worked; and there is no reason to doubt O'Keeffe's cooperation in the management of her career. Stieglitz could not have mounted and sustained the promotional campaign he did without her assent, and the outcome was remarkable. By 1927, ten years after her first one-woman show in New York, critics considered O'Keeffe one of America's most important artists. Moreover, the sales of her work had made her one of its most successful, generating enough income to assure her of being able to continue to devote her life to her work.

But whereas it seems only reasonable that O'Keeffe cooperated in Stieglitz's promotion of her work—and could not have quibbled with its ultimate success—it is clear that she resented the publicity inspired by his contention that her art was the first to symbolize visually female sexual feelings. This notion, applied particularly to her abstractions, was widely adopted by critics in the early 1920s, and at this point in her career it would have been difficult, if not disastrous, for her to challenge it publicly. Her disapproval of it, however, can be demonstrated by examining the shift of emphasis that occurred in her work, in 1923, after her first major exhibition was dominantly reviewed as a celebration of eroticism.

The idea of O'Keeffe as an erotic creature had been convincingly demonstrated by Stieglitz in 1921 in a retrospective exhibition of his own work. O'Keeffe had become Stieglitz's photographic obsession, and his comprehensive "portrait" of her, begun in 1917 and extending over a period of two decades, remains today one of the most accurate indications of what he believed about her as a woman and as an artist. When he included a group of the early photographs of her in his 1921 exhibition, the result was electrifying.[16] As one critic recalled, it "put her at once on the map. Everybody knew the name."[17]

The most controversial of the prints made apparent the intimacy between photographer and model, describing almost every aspect of O'Keeffe with a directness rarely seen in photography to that point. But there were also nude and seminude images of her in which the positions of her arms and hands echoed forms in her abstract drawings, which were included in the background. In establishing explicit correlations between her body and her work, these photographs confirmed the notion Stieglitz had promoted since 1916—that O'Keeffe's sexuality was the source of her expression.

Essays written after the exhibition by Stieglitz's close friends, Marsden Hartley and critic Paul Rosenfeld, extolled O'Keeffe as a sexually liberated woman expressing that liberation in her art. Obviously seeing O'Keeffe through Stieglitz's eyes, Rosenfeld, for example, described her as a "woman polarizing herself, accepting fully the nature long denied, spiritualizing her sex" and went on to describe "great painful and ecstatic climaxes" in her work.[18] Hartley wrote: "The pictures of O'Keeffe . . . are probably as living and shameless private documents as exist."[19]

When Stieglitz presented O'Keeffe's exhibition in 1923—the first of what would be annual exhibitions of her work he sponsored until his death—critics interpreted O'Keeffe's work in his terms. Rosenfeld's pieces, which had been published in widely read periodicals, and Hartley's essay, which Stieglitz reprinted in the exhibition's brochure, were obviously considered definitive assessments of O'Keeffe's art. They set the tone of the reviews, and the critics were probably no less convinced that what had been written about O'Keeffe's art was correct when they read the statement she prepared for the brochure to explain the genesis of her art:

One day seven years ago I found myself saying to myself—I can't live where I want to—I can't go where I want to—I can't do what I want to—I can't even say what I want to—. School and things that painters have taught me even keep me from painting as I want to. I decided I was a very stupid fool not to at least paint as I wanted to and say what I wanted to when I painted as that seemed to be the only thing I could do that didn't concern anybody but myself—that was nobody's business but my own.—So . . . I found that I could say things with color and shapes that I couldn't say in any other way—things that I had no words for.[20]

Although O'Keeffe was attempting to describe how her early training had prevented her from expressing her own ideas and feelings, as well as how she had rejected it in favor of making her own response to reality the inspiration of her art, her statement could be interpreted as an admission that she had overcome a history of confinement or repression and was at last able to express in art what could not be spoken.

There was no checklist of the more than one hundred works exhibited in 1923, but the show was retrospective and documented the diversity of O'Keeffe's ongoing experimentation with self-expression. It included such apparently pure abstractions as *Blue and Green Music*, which is related compositionally to *Special No. 9* and reflects O'Keeffe's continuing efforts to approximate visually her emotional responses to music; semiabstract landscapes, such as *Evening Star III*, which was based directly on an experience in the Texas plains; as well as closely observed still lifes she made in the early 1920s (fig. 3). But the works without recognizable subject matter attracted the attention of most reviewers, who considered them important indications of the nature of the artist herself. As one critic summarized the exhibition:

3. *Apple Family III*. 1921. Oil on canvas, 8 x 11". Private collection

"These emotional abstractions . . . seem to be a clear case of Freudian suppressed desires in paint. She admits that she has never done anything she wanted to do. . . or even painted anything she wanted to until she painted as she is painting now. So, undoubtedly the work is in the way of being an escape. She sublimates herself in her art."[21]

Letters O'Keeffe wrote at the time document that she was not pleased with the 1923 reviews, which almost uniformly assessed her work in terms of what it revealed about her "female" nature. But she could not have objected simply to the idea that her art contained a female component. In 1916 she described a "woman's feeling" she found in it, and as late as 1930 she confirmed that, as a painter, she was expressing her femaleness when she stated: "Before I put brush to canvas, I question 'Is this mine? Is it all intrinsically of myself? Is it influenced by some idea or some photograph of an idea which I acquired from some man?'

. . . I am trying with all my skill to do painting that is all of a woman, as well as all of me."[22]

What she objected to in the 1923 reviews was the idea that had been implied by critics since the late 1910s—that she used her art to liberate her repressed sexual feelings, thereby symbolizing the female erotic experience. That she disagreed with assessments of herself as a "liberated" female is clear in a letter she wrote the fall before her 1923 show opened in which she disclaimed Hartley's and Rosenfeld's opinions to a friend: "You see Rosenfeld's articles have embarrassed me—[and] I wanted to lose the one for the Hartley book when I had the only copy of it to read—so it couldn't be in the book. The things they write sound so strange and far removed from what I feel of myself."[23] But her displeasure with the 1923 reviews is perhaps best demonstrated by the decisions she made about the work she intended to show the following year.

Recognizing that her abstractions had been most susceptible to Freudian interpretations in 1923, she determined to make the work in her 1924 exhibition, as she put it, "as objective as I can."[24] The checklist of paintings shown that year reflects her resolve. Of fifty-one works, only three were listed as "Abstractions"; and the exhibitions that followed in the 1920s were dominated by works with obvious still-life, landscape, or architectural subject matter. (The extent to which O'Keeffe remained affected by the reception of her abstract works in 1923 is indicated by the fact that most of her formative abstractions were excluded from subsequent exhibitions of her work until the 1950s.)

Thus, after the 1923 exhibition, in an attempt to dispel the idea that the origin of her expression as a female artist was her sexuality, O'Keeffe saturated her imagery with forms whose source in the visible world is relatively unequivocal. And for the rest of her life, whether working in New York, where she lived year-round until 1929, or in New Mexico, where she worked in the summers for two decades before moving there permanently in 1949, the art she produced is overwhelmingly representational, characterized by elements drawn from her immediate environment. *Radiator Building, Night, New York* for example, is a response to the new skyscrapers that were being built near the Shelton Hotel, where she lived winters from 1925 to 1936; *White Canadian Barn II* is one of several paintings of architectural forms she observed during an extended trip to the Gaspé Peninsula; the imagery in *Hills and Mesa to the West* and *Winter Cottonwoods East V* (plate 16) was derived directly from landscape forms near her houses in New Mexico.

O'Keeffe did not abandon making abstractions, but with few exceptions those she completed after the 1923 show are more obviously related to forms she saw around her than those she completed from the mid-1910s through the early 1920s.[25] Her later abstractions frequently resulted from increasing simplifications within serial interpretations of a single subject. *Jack-in-the-Pulpit V* (plate 8), for example, is one of seven paintings of the jack-in-the-pulpit flower that grew at Lake George, New York, where she painted part of each year into the 1930s; *Black Place Green* (plate 12) is from a group of at least twelve paintings of an area of dark hills in the Navajo country of northwestern New Mexico that she discovered in the 1940s; *Patio Door—Green-Red* (plate 13) is one of at least twenty-four paintings she made of one of the doors at her house in Abiquiu, New Mexico. Although one series of paintings she completed late in her career, which includes *It Was Red and Pink* (plate 15), appears to recapture the apparent spontaneity of her early abstractions (see plates 2 and 3), O'Keeffe made it clear that the series evolved from the experience of airplane flight and represented "rivers seen from the air."[26] Similarly, she directly attributed the forms in *Sky Above Clouds IV* (plate 14), her largest work—made when she was almost eighty years old—to a visual experience she had while in flight.

But in most of O'Keeffe's work after the mid-1920s, the relationship between forms and their sources in the visible world is obvious. Her choice of subject matter, along with her increasingly dispassionate treatment and meticulous presentation of it, was noticed by several critics in the late 1920s who decried the "bodilessness" of her work, faulted it for approaching the "photographic," or called it "clinical" and "intellectual." Among paintings of this period are such magnified views of flowers as *Black Iris III*.

O'Keeffe's "large flowers" were first exhibited in 1925, shortly after she decided to remove ambiguity from her imagery by concentrating on "objective" painting. Despite her intentions, however, the imagery in these paintings is ambiguous enough to have provoked continuing controversy about their meaning, and probably as a result they remain her most popular works. She remarked later that she had hoped the "large flowers" would attract attention to her work because they were made up of small forms enlarged to many times their actual size; but as flower forms can suggest the forms of human sexual anatomy, they attracted attention of a very different order. In the relative absence of abstractions from her exhibitions after 1923, critics who were convinced that O'Keeffe's work had sexual content shifted their readings of it to the magnified flowers and continued to offer Freudian interpretations of her art.

O'Keeffe kept making and exhibiting the flower paintings, despite their critical reception, and among the many possible reasons that she did so, the most probable is that the paintings had indeed attracted the kind of attention she believed they would: they were very popular with her patrons. By the late 1930s, when the demand for her work had made her financially independent and her position in the New York art world was beyond compromise, she finally took issue publicly with a major premise of Stieglitz's continuing promotion of her work by declaring that there was no erotic content in her flower paintings. For the catalogue of her 1939 show, she wrote: "Well—I made you take time to look at what I saw and when you took time to really notice my flower you hung all your own associations with flowers on my flower and you write about my flower as if I think and see what you think and see of the flower—and I don't."[27] And although she made clear what she did not intend her flowers to mean, she did nothing to suggest what she did intend them to mean. In fact, she never chose to explain her work, typically stating, as she did in 1968: "If you don't get it, that's too bad. There's nothing more to say than what I painted."[28]

But regardless of what she stated or did not state about her work, because of the type of image and subject matter O'Keeffe chose to work with after the mid-1920s, historians have associated her with other artists working in the 1920s and 1930s, including the Precisionists (also called the Immaculates or the Cubist-Realists) and the Surrealists.[29]

4. *Black Rock with Blue Sky and White Clouds*. 1972. Oil on canvas, 36 x 31¼". Alfred Stieglitz Collection, Bequest of Georgia O'Keeffe, 1987.250.3. Photograph courtesy The Art Institute of Chicago

Indeed, there are superficial relationships between some O'Keeffes and the types of works that characterize these groups. For example, the forms in *Radiator Building, Night, New York* resemble the subject matter and delineation associated with the Precisionists. The highly arbitrary juxtapositions and spatial manipulations in *Black Cross with Red Sky*, *Deer's Skull with Pedernal*, and *Pelvis with Shadows and the Moon* (plate 10) could be related to similar devices in Surrealism. But there have been no convincing arguments that link her work with any contemporary movement, and indeed O'Keeffe regularly denied such affiliations. She always considered herself apart from categorization and even resisted exhibiting her work in shows that might associate it with any group, including, late in her life, shows that were organized to acknowledge the accomplishments of women artists. She declared that she was not a woman artist, she was an artist.

O'Keeffe succeeded in promoting herself as an independent, a loner, and a pioneer, particularly after she moved to the remoteness of northern New Mexico in the late 1940s. From then until the 1970s, when failing eyesight forced her to quit painting, she continued to present immediately recognizable subject matter, or she abstracted from it as she had since the mid-1920s and, in the process, created the inventive and distinctively personal body of work we know her for today. The character of her very late painting is summarized in *Black Rock with Blue Sky and White Clouds* (fig. 4). The painting's single rock, enlarged and isolated like a piece of sculpture on a plinth, is seen against the Southwestern sky O'Keeffe had celebrated for years and suggests the reconciliation she had made between nature and abstraction. In fact, her mature work, though fully realized within the expressive limitations she set for it, exists in a tenuous space between two major and opposing trends in twentieth-century American painting, abstractionism and realism.

Had she continued, however, to work as freely with abstraction after 1923 as she had before, rather than attempting to dissociate her art from Freudian interpretations by making it as "objective" as she could, she might instead have continued to develop the direction of her early work and become one of America's foremost abstractionists.

NOTES

1. Arthur Wesley Dow, *Composition* (New York: Doubleday-Page & Company, 1913), p. 5. She had read about this idea in Kandinsky's *Concerning the Spiritual in Art*.
2. Bob Groves, "Georgia O'Keeffe and the Color of Music: For More Than a Decade, Santa Fe Chamber Music Festival Performers and the Famous Artist Gave Each Other the Gift of Art," *Impact: Albuquerque Journal Magazine* (28 July 1987), p. 5. Grammar and punctuation errors in O'Keeffe citations have been corrected.
3. O'Keeffe to Anita Pollitzer, September 1915, in *Lovingly Georgia: The Complete Correspondence of Georgia O'Keeffe & Anita Pollitzer*, ed. Clive Giboire (New York: Simon & Schuster Inc., 1990), p. 9.
4. Ibid, June 1915, p. 5.
5. "Austere Stripper," *Time* 47 (27 May 1946), p. 74.
6. O'Keeffe to Pollitzer, October 1915, in *Lovingly Georgia*, p. 40.
7. Pollitzer to O'Keeffe, 1 January 1916, in *Lovingly Georgia*, pp. 115–116.
8. Roxana Robinson, who quoted part of what O'Keeffe wrote in *Georgia O'Keeffe: A Life* (New York: Harper & Row, 1989), p. 130, has generously provided me with the additional phrase included here.
9. O'Keeffe to Pollitzer, October 1915, in *Lovingly Georgia*, p. 71.
10. Ibid, January 1916, p. 124.
11. Henri Bergson, "What is the Object of Art?" *Camera Work* 37 (January 1912), pp. 23–24.
12. Alfred Stieglitz, "Woman in Art," in Dorothy Norman, *Alfred Stieglitz: An American Seer* (New York: Random House, 1973), p. 136.
13. [Alfred Stieglitz], "Georgia O'Keeffe, C. Duncan, Réné [sic] Lafferty,"*Camera Work* 48 (October 1916), p. 12. Reprinted in Barbara Buhler Lynes, *O'Keeffe, Stieglitz and the Critics, 1916–1929* (Ann Arbor: UMI Research Press, 1989; reprint, Chicago: University of Chicago Press, 1991), Appendix A, no. 2 (hereafter referred to as *OS*).
14. Henry Tyrrell, "New York Art Exhibition and Gallery Notes: Esoteric Art at '291,'" *The Christian Science Monitor* (4 May 1917), p. 4. Reprinted in *OS*, Appendix A, no. 3.
15. For an excellent discussion of these influences, see Sarah Whitaker Peters, *Becoming O'Keeffe: The Early Years* (New York: Abbeville Press, 1991).
16. For representative examples of Stieglitz's early photographs of O'Keeffe, see *Georgia O'Keeffe: A Portrait by Alfred Stieglitz* (New York: Metropolitan Museum of Art, 1978).
17. Henry McBride, "O'Keeffe at the Museum: An Exhibition that Confirms the Opinion Long Held by the Public," *New York Sun* (18 May 1946), p. 9.
18. Paul Rosenfeld, "American Painting," *Dial* 71 (December 1921), p. 666. This and Rosenfeld's other essays are reprinted in *OS*, Appendix A, nos. 6, 8, and 28.
19. See Marsden Hartley, "Georgia O'Keeffe," from "Some Women Artists in Modern Painting," chap. 13 in *Adventures in the Arts* (New York: Boni and Liveright, 1921; reprint, New York: Hacker Art Books, 1972), p. 116. Partially reprinted in *OS*, Appendix A, no. 5.
20. Georgia O'Keeffe, statement in *Alfred Stieglitz Presents One Hundred Pictures: Oils, Watercolors, Pastels, Drawings by Georgia O'Keeffe, American* [exhibition brochure] (New York: The Anderson Galleries, 29 January–10 February 1923), n.p. Reprinted in *OS*, Appendix A, no. 11.
21. Helen Appleton Read, "Georgia O'Keeffe's Show an Emotional Escape," *Brooklyn Daily Eagle* (11 February 1923), 2B. Reprinted in *OS*, Appendix A, no. 17.
22. O'Keeffe to Pollitzer, 4 January 1916, in *Lovingly Georgia*, p. 117; and Gladys Oaks, "Radical Writer and Woman Artist Clash on Propaganda and Its Uses," *The [New York] World* (16 March 1930), Women's section, 1, 3.
23. O'Keeffe to Mitchell Kennerley, fall 1922, in Jack Cowart, Juan Hamilton, and Sarah Greenough, *Georgia O'Keeffe: Art and Letters* (Washington, D.C.: National Gallery of Art, 1987), letter 26 (hereafter referred to as *AL*).
24. O'Keeffe to Sherwood Anderson, 11 February 1924, in *AL*, letter 30.
25. Lisa Mintz Messinger also made this point in *Georgia O'Keeffe* (New York: Thames and Hudson; Metropolitan Museum of Art, 1988), pp. 41–42.
26. Georgia O'Keeffe, *Georgia O'Keeffe* (New York: Viking Press, 1976), opp. ill. 103.
27. Georgia O'Keeffe, statement in *Georgia O'Keeffe: Exhibition of Oils and Pastels* [exh. catalogue] (New York: An American Place, 22 January–17 March 1939). Photocopy in National Gallery of Art, Washington, D.C., Gallery Archives, RG 17B. For a discussion of O'Keeffe's response to feminist interpretations of her flower paintings, see Barbara Buhler Lynes, "O'Keeffe and Feminism: A Problem of Position," in *The Expanding Discourse: Feminism and Art History*, eds. Norma Broude and Mary D. Garrard (New York: HarperCollins, 1992).
28. Edith Evans Asbury, "Silent Desert Still Charms Georgia O'Keeffe, Near 81," *The New York Times* (2 November 1968), p. 30.
29. See, for example, Milton W. Brown, "Cubist-Realism: An American Style," *Marsyas* 3 (1943–1945), pp. 139–160, *American Painting: from the Armory Show to the Depression* (Princeton: Princeton University Press, 1955), pp. 126–280; John I. H. Baur, *Revolution and Tradition in Modern American Art* (Cambridge: Harvard University Press, 1951), pp. 59–60; and Martin L. Friedman, *The Precisionist View in American Art* (Minneapolis: Walker Art Center, 1960). Yet it has become increasingly clear that O'Keeffe's work resists this and other categorizations. See Abraham A. Davidson's *Early American Modernist Painting: 1910–1936* (New York: Harper & Row, Publishers, 1981), where O'Keeffe's work is included in chapters variously entitled "The Stieglitz Group," "Color Painters," "Precisionism," and "The Independents." See also Peters, *Becoming O'Keeffe*, pp. 209, 300.

FURTHER READING

Cowart, Jack, Juan Hamilton, and Sarah Greenough. *Georgia O'Keeffe: Art and Letters*. Washington, D.C.: National Gallery of Art, 1987.

Eldredge, Charles C., III. *Georgia O'Keeffe*. New York: Abrams, 1991.

Lisle, Laurie. *Portrait of an Artist: A Biography of Georgia O'Keeffe*. New York: Seaview Books, 1980; rev. ed., New York: Washington Square Press, 1987.

Lynes, Barbara Buhler. "O'Keeffe and Feminism: A Problem of Position." In *The Expanding Discourse, Feminism and Art History*, eds. Norma Broude and Mary D. Garrard. New York: HarperCollins, 1992.

——————. *O'Keeffe, Stieglitz and the Critics: 1916–1929*. Ann Arbor: UMI Research Press, 1989; reprint Chicago: University of Chicago Press, 1991.

Messinger, Lisa Mintz. *Georgia O'Keeffe*. New York: Thames and Hudson; Metropolitan Museum of Art, 1988.

O'Keeffe, Georgia. *Georgia O'Keeffe*. New York: Viking Press, 1976.

Peters, Sarah Whitaker. *Becoming O'Keeffe: The Early Years*. New York: Abbeville Press, 1991.

Robinson, Roxana. *Georgia O'Keeffe: A Life*. New York: Harper & Row, 1989.

The publisher wishes to acknowledge Elizabeth Glassman, president, Judy Lopez, and Melanie Crowley of the Georgia O'Keeffe Foundation for their help with this publication.

First published in 1993 in the United States of America by Rizzoli International Publications, Inc.
300 Park Avenue South
New York, New York 10010

Library of Congress Cataloging-in-Publication Data
Lynes, Barbara Buhler, 1942–
　　Georgia O'Keeffe/by Barbara Buhler Lynes.
　　　　p.　cm. — (Rizzoli art series)
　　Includes bibliographical references (p
　　ISBN 0-8478-1650-8
　　1. O'Keeffe, Georgia 1887–1986
　　I. O'Keeffe, Georgia 1887–1986. I
　　ND6537.039L96　1993
　　759.13—dc20

Plate 2 photograph by Paul Hes[...]
Plates 5, 6, 8, 11, and fig. 3 ph[...]
N.Y. ©1987
Plate 12 photograph by Steven[...]

Series Editor: Norma Broude[...]
Series designed by José Co[...]

Printed in Italy

Front cover: see colorpla[...]

Index to Colorplates

1. *Evening Star III*. 1917. Made while O'Keeffe was teaching art in Canyon, Texas, this watercolor is one of eight works in which the same subject is similarly treated. The group displays her early interest in working serially.

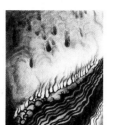

2. *Special No. 9*. 1915. This abstract drawing, which was among the first of her works exhibited by Alfred Stieglitz in 1916, resulted from O'Keeffe's decision to free her imagery from the influences of her academic training.

3. *Blue and Green Music*. 1919. *Blue and Green Music* and other paintings similarly titled from 1919, such as *Music Pink and Blue I* and *Music Pink and Blue II*, demonstrate O'Keeffe's keen interest at that time in exploring relationships between color and music.

4. *Grey Line with Lavender and Yellow*. c.1923. Among the numerous abstractions that O'Keeffe completed in the early 1920s, this work is a fully realized example of her determination to give her feelings visual form.

5. *Black Iris III*. 1926. Completed the year after O'Keeffe's "large flowers" were first exhibited, this painting has become one of her best-known works.

6. *Radiator Building, Night, New York*. 1927. O'Keeffe began painting New York buildings in the mid-1920s, at about the same time that she and Stieglitz moved into one of the city's newest and tallest residential hotels, the Shelton (now the Marriott East Side).

7. *Black Cross with Red Sky*. 1929. Painted in response to her first summer in New Mexico, *Black Cross with Red* ̷̷y embodies O'Keeffe's response to ̷ experiences there. She wrote: "I saw ̷crosses so often—like a thin dark ̷ f the Catholic church spread over ̷w Mexico landscape."

̷-the-Pulpit V*. 1930. O'Keeffe ̷ncreasingly abstract paint- ̷ack-in-the-pulpit flower that ̷ Lake George, New York, ̷rked part of each year ̷o the 1930s.

9. *Deer's Skull with Pedernal*. 1936. This painting juxtaposes two forms that O'Keeffe came to know well in New Mexico: an animal skull that she probably found in the desert and the Pedernal, the flat-topped mountain that dominates the view to the south from her Ghost Ranch house.

10. *Pelvis with Shadows and the Moon*. 1943. The seemingly exotic subject matter in this and many related paintings of the 1930s and 1940s is derived directly from O'Keeffe's everyday experience in the Southwest, yet it has motivated historians to link her work with Surrealism.

11. *Hills and Mesa to the West*. 1945. The brilliant colors found in landscape forms near O'Keeffe's Ghost Ranch house in New Mexico inspired many of her paintings of the 1940s.

12. *Black Place Green*. 1949. O'Keeffe was fascinated by an area of grey black landscape forms in the Navajo country of northwestern New Mexico that she discovered in the 1940s and made it the subject of at least twelve paintings.

13. *Patio Door—Green-Red*. 1951. O'Keeffe often claimed that she bought her house in Abiquiu, New Mexico, purely because of her interest in one of its doors, which is represented in this and at least twenty-four of her other paintings.

14. *Sky Above Clouds IV*. 1965. Airplane flight also inspired this painting—O'Keeffe's largest—which she began when she was almost eighty.

15. *It Was Red and Pink*. 1959. This painting of river forms was inspired by O'Keeffe's fascination with landscape configurations seen while flying in an airplane.

16. *Winter Cottonwoods East V*. 1954. This relatively "soft image" is one of many studies of the cottonwood trees that grow in the Chama River Valley, which can be seen from O'Keeffe's Abiquiu studio.

1. *Evening Star III*. 1917. Watercolor on paper, 9 x 11⁷/₈". Collection, The Museum of Modern Art, New York. Mr. and Mrs. Donald B. Straus Fund. Photograph ©1992, The Museum of Modern Art, New York

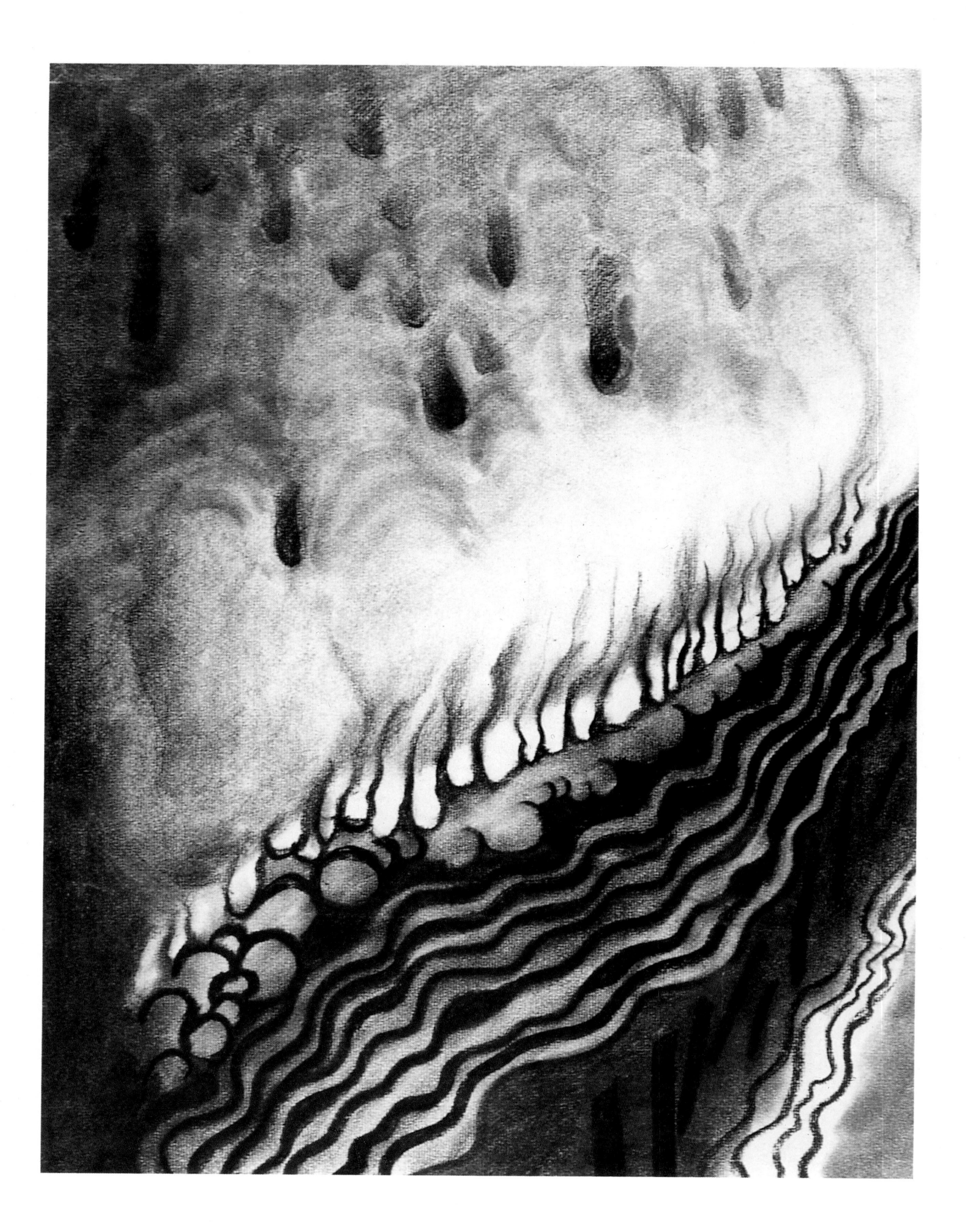

2. *Special No. 9.* 1915. Charcoal on paper, 24 x 12¼".
Courtesy of The Menil Collection, Houston, Texas

3. *Blue and Green Music*. 1919. Oil on canvas, 23 x 19". Alfred Stieglitz Collection.
gift of Georgia O'Keeffe, 1969.835. Photograph courtesy The Art Institute of Chicago

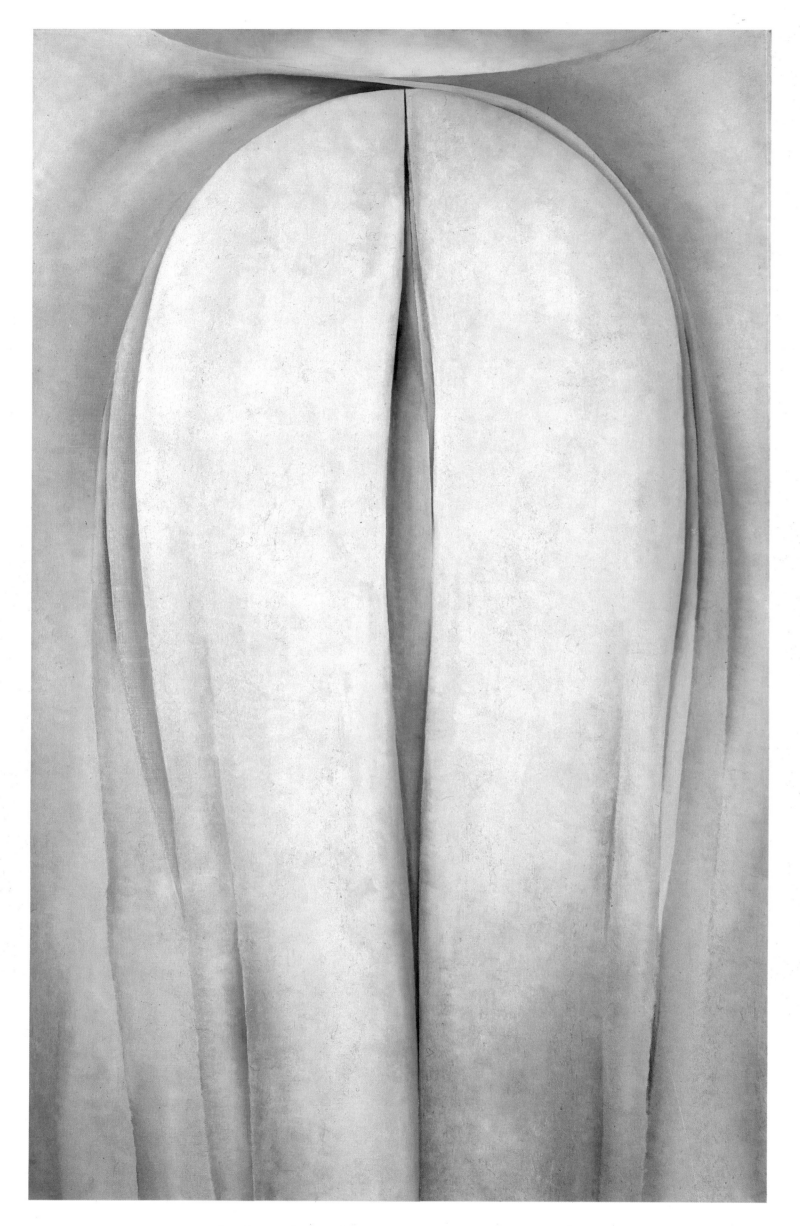

4. *Grey Line with Lavender and Yellow.* c.1923. Oil on canvas, 48 x 30".
The Metropolitan Museum of Art, Alfred Stieglitz Collection, Bequest of Georgia O'Keeffe, 1986

5. *Black Iris III*. 1926. Oil on canvas, 36 x 29⁷/8".
The Metropolitan Museum of Art, Alfred Stieglitz Collection, 1969

6. *Radiator Building, Night, New York*. 1927. Oil on canvas, 48 x 30".
Carl Van Vechten Gallery of Fine Arts, Fisk University, Nashville

7. *Black Cross with Red Sky*. 1929. Oil on canvas, 40 x 32".
Photograph courtesy the Collection of Mr. and Mrs. Gerald P. Peters, Santa Fe, New Mexico

9. *Deer's Skull with Pedernal*. 1936. Oil on canvas, 36 x 30".
Gift of the William H. Lane Foundation. Courtesy, Museum of Fine Arts, Boston

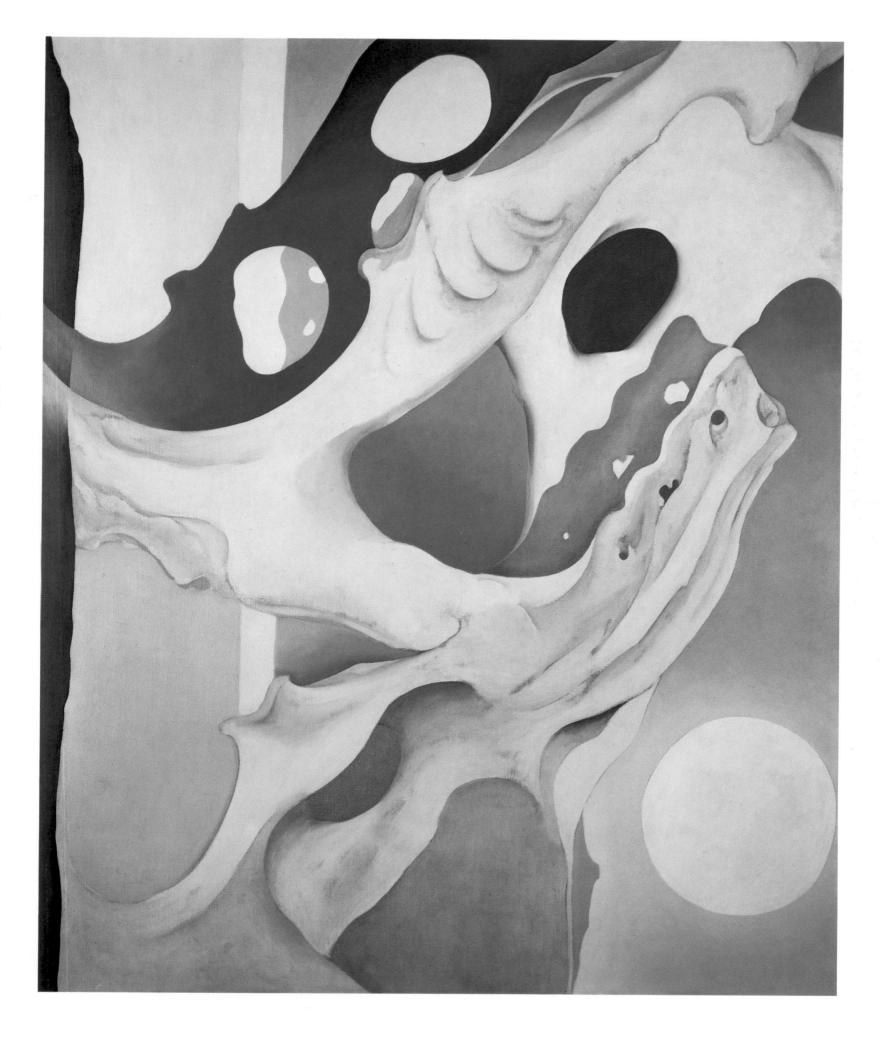

10. *Pelvis with Shadows and the Moon.* 1943. Oil on canvas, 40 x 48³/₄".
Private Collection. Courtesy Joan T. Washburn Gallery, New York

11. *Hills and Mesa to the West.* 1945. Oil on canvas, 19 x 36".
Private Collection

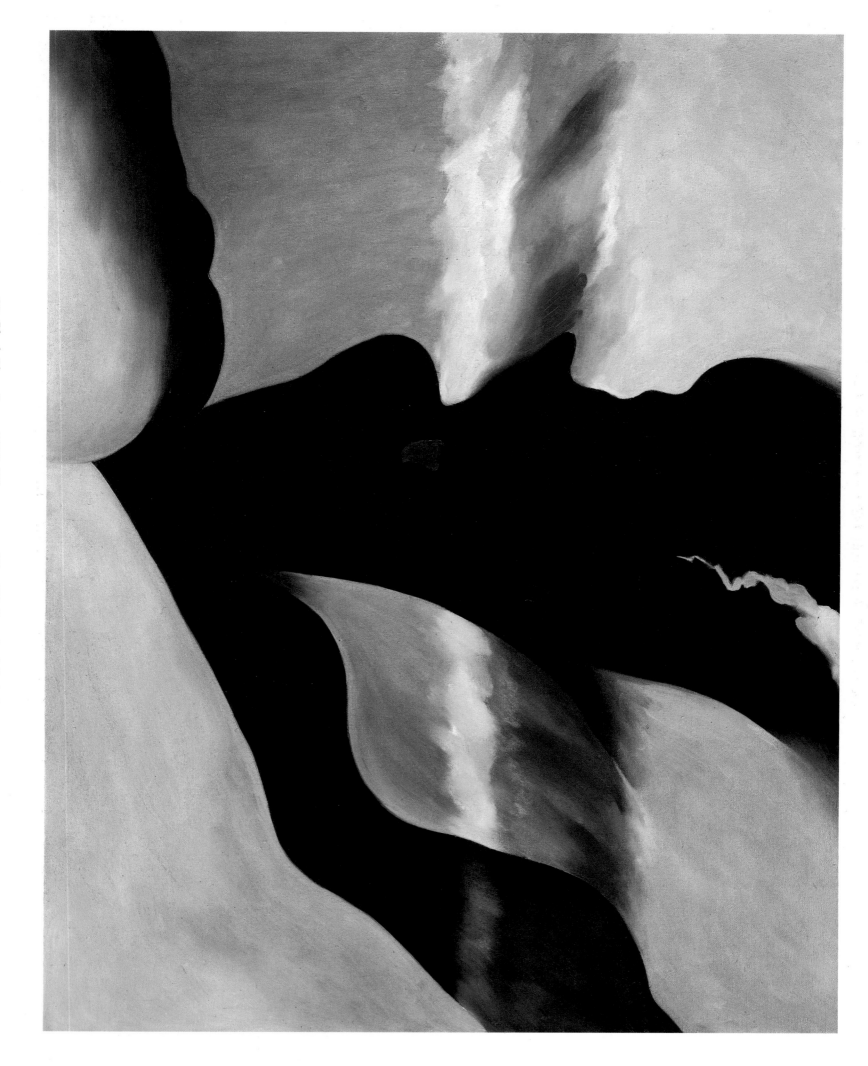

12. *Black Place Green.* 1949. Oil on canvas, 38 x 48″. Promised 50th Anniversary
Gift of an anonymous donor. Whitney Museum of American Art P 17 79

13. *Patio Door—Green-Red.* 1951. Oil on canvas, 12 x 26".
Photograph courtesy Gerald Peters Gallery, Santa Fe, New Mexico

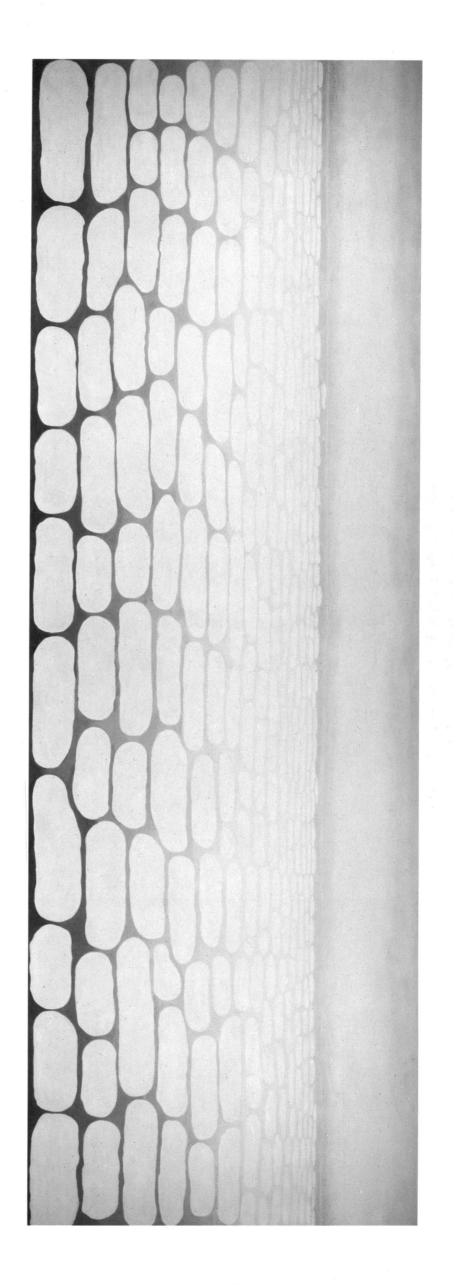

14. *Sky Above Clouds IV.* 1965. Oil on canvas, 100 x 299". Restricted gift of the Paul and Gabriella Rosenbaum Foundation, gift of Georgia O'Keeffe, 1983.821. Photograph courtesy The Art Institute of Chicago.

15. *It Was Red and Pink*. 1959. Oil on canvas, 30 x 40".
Milwaukee Art Museum, Gift of Mrs. Harry Lynde Bradley

16. *Winter Cottonwoods East V*. 1954. Oil on canvas, 40 x 30".
Photograph courtesy Gerald Peters Gallery, Santa Fe, New Mexico